How to Improve Your Relationship With Your Father
Have the relationship with your Mother that you've always wanted

By Jean Young

EXPERIENCE
EVERYTHING
P U B L I S H I N G

Disclaimer

This document is geared towards providing exact and reliable information in regards to the topic and issue covered. The publication is sold with the idea that the publisher is not required to render accounting, officially permitted, or otherwise, qualified services. If advice is necessary, legal or professional, a practiced individual in the profession should be ordered.

- From a Declaration of Principles which was accepted and approved equally by a Committee of the American Bar Association and a Committee of Publishers and Associations:

The information provided herein is stated to be truthful and consistent, in that any liability, in terms of inattention or otherwise, by any usage or abuse of any policies, processes, or directions contained within is the solitary and utter responsibility of the recipient reader. Under no circumstances will any legal responsibility or blame be held against the publisher for any reparation, damages, or monetary loss due to the information herein, either directly or indirectly.

The information herein is offered for informational purposes solely, and is universal as so. The presentation of the information is without contract or any type of guarantee assurance.

The trademarks that are used are without any consent, and the publication of the trademark is without permission or backing by the trademark owner. All trademarks and brands within this book are for clarifying purposes only and are the owned by the owners themselves, not affiliated with this document.

Introduction

Growing up, we have always had our fathers to look up to, to play with, to protect us, to teach us and so many other things. Sometimes a father does not get as much credit in the parenting world because most often than not, raising a child is often a task attributed to the mother. Nevertheless, a father is just as important as the mother when it comes to raising kids.

If we were in the perfect world, no child would grow up without his biological father by his side. In this perfect world, there would be nothing but great memories, happy days and loving family members surrounding a child.

There would be no verbal, physical or emotional abuse. Parents, both mom and dad, would be awesome at handling the kids, family life, work and their relationship with their spouse. No one will ever have to experience the sad realities of life. But unfortunately, the perfect world only exists in our minds.

Take a look around you. You see fathers leaving their unborn children. Some might be there physically but their presence does not have any significance. Some are only there for the good times but are never able to support their kids through the difficult times. There are some who even go to the point of abusing their kids. Disgusting as it may sound, there are despicable fathers who beat their kids up when they make mistakes or sometimes for no reason at all. They had a bad day at work, maybe an argument with someone or are either drunk or high on drugs and whatever frustration they are feeling are taken out on the kids. What's even more disgusting is that there are fathers who also abuse their daughters or sons sexually. It's safe to say that some fathers are just biological fathers but have nothing to contribute to raising their kids.

But cheer up because not everything in life is sad and gloomy. Even though there are so many fathers who do not live up to their role as a father, there are still quite many who perfectly understand what the role of the father includes. When you look at the brighter side of things, you'll see fathers who are hands-on when it comes to caring for their kids. Some step into the role of being the father of their partner's children from a previous relationship. There are uncles and good family friends too that some kids consider to be their fathers.

So what can we conclude about fathers? Being a father is not just limited to being the sperm donor. A father needs to do much more to be actually considered as a dad. And sometimes you can still be a father to a child despite not being biologically related to each other. So what are the roles of a father in a child's life?

1   *The Protector*

A father should be able to protect his children from any harm. This does not just refer to any physical harm that we are bound to encounter on a daily basis. A father should be able to safeguard the moral values of his children because in the world that we live in today, the lack of moral values has led children to do things that one should not be doing like drug abuse, excessive drinking, lack of respect for others and so on.

2   *The Provider*

In the modern day that we live in today, it is not just the father though that provides financial support for the families since modern day mothers are now contributing too. However, a father must always make sure that he is able to provide the material needs of his family and should also show his children how to live a life that is well within their means. A father should provide financial knowledge and responsibility for his kids.

3 The Teacher

It's not just the teacher that we find in schools that can teach kids something. Children can learn from the experiences of their father and his knowledge as well in various things. A father can show the child what the world is really like and answer the random questions that children ask.

4 The Playmate

From being an infant and well into the teenage years, a father can and will always be a child's first playmate. From peek-a-boos to shooting hoops in the garage, fathers will always be part of a child's play time.

5 The Companion

Spending time with children should always be on top of the priority list of fathers. Being too busy should never be an excuse to hang out with your kids. And even the kids are older, fathers should still be good companions for their kids and grandchildren too.

6 The Trainer and Talent Developer

Kids will always be asking for assurance if they are doing the right things. It is the role of dads to help them out with whatever it is that the kid is trying to learn. Or if a kid exhibits a talent in something, dads should help develop this talent.

7 The Good Role Model

If a father wants his children to grow up as responsible people and good citizens, it is important that he serves as a good example. A person can only be a great leader if he can also be a good follower. And kids being kids, they will eagerly follow whatever it is that they see their parents are doing.

A good and healthy relationship between a father and his kids is really important and should not be taken for granted. When a father is also involved in the parenting of the child, a child will have a wider range of experience when it comes to different personalities because how a father parents a child is different from the ways of a mother. While the mother is often cautious when playing with children, a father will not hesitate to wrestle with his kids or throw them in the air just to make them squeal with joy. Therefore, a child learns how to take risks and be a little more carefree. Fathers help their kids build their confidence too because fathers always push the kids to their limits. Another thing that children can benefit from having a father around is that his vocabulary can be expanded and even his linguistic skills can benefit from it too.

Why? Often, fathers will not simplify their way of communication to make it easier for a child to understand. So instead, they communicate with their kids the same they would communicate with other people thus a child will need to improve his vocabulary and linguistic skills to understand his father. Fathers also have a different method when it comes to instilling discipline in their kids and they help prepare children for the real world too. And with a father around, it is easier for kids to understand the world of men.

For a relationship between a father and a child to go well, it is important that the effort does not only come from the father. Maybe an exception is applicable when a kid is still young. But when you are old enough, it is also important learn to find ways to make the relationship between you and your father. What can you do to help improve your relationship with your father? Well, you will find some tips in the next few sections so keep turning the pages to find out.

The Changes In Fatherhood

When you say father, it could be possible that you are not referring to somebody who bore kids with his spouse, the breadwinner of the family and the disciplinarian. Fathers come in different forms and circumstances now. Although there are still a lot of fathers who are married and breadwinners of the family, being single is no longer a hindrance when it comes to fulfilling one's role as a father. There are gay fathers now and then there are step-fathers. Some people who have taken care of kids because of an illness are considered as fathers too and even guardians are being looked up to as a father figure nowadays.

During the 18th and 19th century, the sole purpose of fathers was to provide financial resources for the family and take care of the family financially.

The role of nurturing a child and providing emotional support was left to the mother. The only reason a father would fail back then was if he was unable to provide this one need for his family. But this does not mean though that a child and father then did not have an emotional bond. It was just shown in a different way compared to dads of today. Instead of showing their love and affection for their children, dads in the past provided approval or disapproval.

But because of the various events and studies that was done, the role of the father changed into something else. A man's parenting capability is no longer solely defined by how well he is able to provide for his family financially but also how involved he is in the family. There is a better understanding now that it is not only mothers that are required for a healthy overall development in a child and that fathers play a big role in it too. Just take a look around you and observe fathers and you'll see the difference. You see fathers playing with their kids, helping kids out in various things, providing advice and so on. There is certainly a huge difference between how fatherhood is seen now and how it was seen before. What are the different things that you can do to help improve the relationship between you and your father? We will now continue discussing that in the next few sections

Section 1: Heart-To-Heart Conversation

You may have had a bad experience with your father or there are some things that you just want to say to him like how he has not been there when you needed him because he was too busy with work. But because you don't have the guts to say it straight in his face, you'd rather keep it inside or blurt it out to other people but not to the person concerned. As a result, the relationship that you have with your father is affected and you start distancing yourself from him. On the surface, you might seem okay but deep inside the gap between you and your dad might be a huge one.

If you want to have a better relationship with your dad then it is about time you stop complaining. Stop ranting to the others about your issues with your dad because no matter how often you rant to them, the problem will not be resolved. The only way you will be able to get things done is to actually talk to the person concerned and that person is no other than your father himself.

Confrontations or heart-to-heart talks are not easy and not everyone has the guts to actually make one happen. But then again, for you to be able to resolve your issues with your father and be on your way to having a better relationship with him then it is important that you find the courage to speak up. Your father is not a mind reader and for him to be aware of what the issue is, you need to voice it out.

Here are some quick tips to help you have a heart-to-heart conversation with your father.

- Find the right timing. The perfect time to pour out your heart is important because you do not want to start discussing such important matters with your dad when he is in the middle of doing something. You need to find a time when both of you are comfortable and relaxed so that it will be easier for both of you to get the conversation going. And also, you need to be in the right place. You do not want to talk in places where so many people can overhear your discussion.

- Begin your conversation that will eventually lead up to what it is you want to talk about. You could say something like *'This is something I've been thinking about....'* or *'I know this is something we have been trying to avoid but I really need to talk to you about this...'*.

Note: Nobody likes conversations that go round and round in circles before getting to the main point so make sure that you are straightforward with your dad.

- Don't be surprised when your father is being stubborn and would start denying things or start avoiding the conversation altogether. So it is important that you tell your father why you need to discuss this matter with him. Once you've pointed out why it is important, let him know how the situation is affecting you and come up with ways to resolve it or how you two should move forward.
- If you notice that your dad has something else preoccupying their mind, then do not hesitate to postpone this discussion with him. Let him know that it's okay and you guys can talk about it at a later time. If you think that your father is also going through problems of his own, get him to talk to you about it and hopefully he will return the favor to you.
- If your father is also going through problem similar to yours then share to him whatever it is that you have in mind as a solution or proposition then you can tell him that hopefully he will do the same for you.
- Do not forget to let your father know that you value him, his time and his advice over other people.

A heart-to-heart conversation with your father might be all you need to get the issues out of the way and have a better relationship with your father. But of course you need to remember that this is a conversation. That means that you should not only be doing the talking but also listen to what your father has to say.

Section 2: Avoid Expecting Perfection

Maybe the reason why your relationship with your father is going through a tough time is because of the expectations that you have set for him and your relationship. Who does not want the perfect father? Who does not want a father that can give you everything that you want and understand what you are going through without you having to say anything? Who does not want a father who stands by you despite everything awful that you have done and keep encouraging you to be better? We all want a father that will give us the freedom that we all long for especially during our teenage years. A father who will not question our choices and decisions. With a perfect father, we will have the perfect relationship too.

But then again, we are not living in the perfect world. We all have flaws and shortcomings. Sometimes we fail to understand the other and sometimes it is hard to accept the reality. And as you can see, the kind of relationship that your friends have with their own fathers does not mean that you'll have the same. You, your father, your friends and their fathers all have unique personalities. This is the very reason why the relationship between you and your father will never be the same kind of relationship that others have. It will be different because you are different from them.

You need to accept the fact that your father will still make mistakes even though he is much older so you expect him to have enough experience and knowledge. He's not perfect. There will be times when he will be too stubborn to hear you out and let you make decisions on your own. In his eyes, you will always be his little child no matter how big you've grown already and no matter how old you are. When he makes mistakes, gently point it out to him and help him correct it instead of going all crazy about it.

When you expect something from your dad, set it to something that you would expect from yourself. If you want your dad to respect you, then do the same to him. If you want him to give you enough space, then make sure that it is something that he can expect from you. Do not ask him for things that you cannot give. It would be quite ironic if you do that. After all, how can you expect someone to give you something that you cannot give.

So again, it's okay to set expectations for your dad and your relationship with him. But please make it realistic.

Section 3: Forgive And Forget

If you know that you are angry at your father or you resent him for some reason, it is really important that you learn to let go of these negative feelings if you want to move forward with your relationship with him. How can you keep going forward if you keep looking back at the past? Stop thinking about the times when he left you and missed out on all the important events of your life. Stop dwelling on how he never appreciated your efforts to please him and how he never spent any time with you. None of these will help at all.

These feelings can be discussed with your father. Maybe, just maybe, he has a reason behind why he acted in such a manner. Although there are things that cannot be justified at all, open your mind and heart to the possibility of putting an end to such negative feelings. Learn to accept that all of that is part of the past now and nothing will ever change that. Dwelling on that will not do any of you any good. However, how the present and the future will go will depend on how much you are willing to forgive and move on.

Yes, it is not easy to just forgive a man who walked out on you or made you feel like you were never good enough.

This is especially true when the man happens to be your father who was supposed to be there as you grew up. But then again, you cannot change things. Think instead of why it is important for you to rebuild your relationship with him and turn it into something better. When you let yourself forgive him for anything that he has done to you, you are freeing yourself from the excess emotional baggage. You'll feel much better in the end. So you will not only be doing your dad a favor but you will also be doing it for yourself. What's the point of hurting about something from the past over and over again, right?

Section 4: Acknowledge His Point Of View

Even though some of your genes comes from him, it does not mean that you will also see things in the same light. You, being much younger than him and less experienced, would probably see things in a different way that he did. On the other hand, he has already gone through so many things in life and is wise enough to know what's right from wrong, at least most of the time. For example, he may tell you not to date someone and you may find it hard to understand.

Remember that the way he sees things are different from how you see the same things. Remember how you used to enjoy certain things when you were younger but now that you are older, your tastes have changed or you look at things differently? Some of those things seem funny and some of those things just seem utterly disgusting or something like that. The same thing applies to your father. The things you do now may seem like the best but he has been there before and he definitely knows all about it.

You may also think that how you were brought up by your father sucked but for him, he thinks he brought you up perfectly well. Again, how you view things and what you think is best will not be the same opinion for your father. There are different things and circumstances that may also be affecting his choices when it comes to bringing you up. But don't hate him for it. Instead, learn to respect his point of view and he will do the same for you.

Section 5: Communicate

You do not need to be in touch with him every hour of the day. Sometimes you do not even need to be in touch with him daily. But it is still important that you stay in touch often enough so that you do not miss out on any important details in his life and neither will he. With the advancement in the current technology, staying in touch is not a problem anymore and there are many ways to keep in touch.

If you have parents who feel that they are too old to be using cellphones, tablets and computer then there is always the telephone to call him on or sending him a letter, post card and birthday card through the mail. But if your father has no qualms about dealing with gadgets, then there are more choices for you to stay in touch. Aside from the old ways, you can send him a text message and call him on his cellphone so even when he is out you can still have a nice chat. To make it seem like you are talking to each other face to face then video calls are an option too. So you see, staying in touch is not a problem anymore.

You and your father need not share every single detail in your life or to be best of friends in order for you to have a good relationship. And again, no need to be calling each other daily. Workout a schedule with your dad that will be convenient for both of you. What's most important is that you and your father have time for each other to just sit and talk, whether it be in person or through phone calls.

Now there will be times when the two of you will not agree on something. Do not start or ensue an argument with him. Instead of doing that, calmly explain to him your stand on the issue so that he'll understand. And of course, be willing to listen to what he has to say because he might actually be pointing out a good point that you might not have thought about.

Section 6: Get To Know Your Father

Wait, what? So you are probably asking why you need to do this. Of course you know your father. You know his name, birthday, where he works, his kids' names, where he lives and stuff like that. But beyond the most obvious details, do you really know your father? What does he like? What is he afraid of? What's his favorite color? How did he and your mom meet? What was his childhood like? What were the things he used to do?

Now while there are some things that you would rather not know like the more intimate details of your father's life, it would be a good idea to really get to know him.

Get to know him beyond just being your father. Know who he is as a person. Sometimes it is awkward to just ask him random questions. It feels like you are being an intruder. So you do not really need to know him in one sitting. You could maybe try to observe him and see what kind of details you can get. Ask him a question every now and then to learn about these details about him. Or even better, why not play a game with him where you can ask each other questions. Now that should be fun.

Aside from asking your father questions, what other tips are there if you want to get to know them better?

- Make sure that the setting is right. You do not need to be sitting across each other when you are asking your father your questions. Instead, casually throw in a question when it feels right.
- The answer to the question that you just asked your father might lead to another story or even another topic. Sometimes, you cannot just help but try to steer the conversation back to the original topic. But don't. Resist the urge to do this and be flexible enough to let your father continue with whatever it is he is saying. Who knows? Maybe the conversation will lead to something even more interesting than you originally asked.

- If you are going to ask your father about things that are quite sensitive you might want to start asking something like '*Dad, I have a question for you and I hope you do not mind me asking...*'
- Be tactful enough when you respond to his answers. Do not ever be rude to him and do not insult your father because of the answer he just gave you. Whatever tactless comment you have, keep it in your mind. Doing so will only prevent your father from telling you further details about him.

You know, you are really never too old to start getting to know your father. It is going to be an easier task to complete when you are still living under the same roof. But even when you are no longer living together, you can still do it as long as you have time to be with him for a chitchat.

Section 7: Make Your Feel Dad Wanted

So your father never tells you that he loves you or is not affectionate enough to show that he cares. But this does not mean that you should also do the same thing to him. As his child, you can do him a favor by showing him that you love him and care for him. 'I love you' is not a phrase that can be said to your partner only. If you love your dad, then let him know.

Your father may not be able to drop everything that he is doing so that he can be there for you at a moment's notice. Or maybe your father might be a little too old for him to help you out with things at home. But if you want your dad to feel wanted and loved, make him feel that you still depend on him even if it is just a little. We're not talking about financial dependence here or continuing to live under his wing. Instead, you could ask for his advice or opinion on things.

Section 8: Be A Better Child

You are probably blaming your father for why the relationship between you and him are not that great. You probably wish that he was richer so that you would have had a more comfortable life or that he was smarter and all the other things that you wished your dad could be. But instead of thinking about it this way, why not take a different approach? Have you ever thought about being a better child for your dad?

So how exactly do you do that? Start thinking about the different things you might have done wrong to him. Instead of just thinking about what you want, learn to be more sensitive about his needs. Do not make things difficult for him and if what he wants is not something that is going to end up in a life and death situation, then give in to what he wants. Your dad, just like any other parent, will probably not ask for help from you unless he has been cornered. Do not wait for that to happen. Think of the possible things that he might need help in.

If your dad just bought a new computer or phone but is not too tech-savvy, then offer to help him learn how to navigate his way with his new gadget. Make it a priority to see them at least once a week if you do not live with him anymore and have dinner together. If you can do it more often than once a week then that would be even better. And during those times that you won't be able to see him, talk to him every now and then just so he is aware that you are thinking of him. If you still live with your dad, then make it a point to abide by the rules that he has set.

When you are trying to be a better child, you do not really need to follow the expectations he has set for the ideal child. It is still important that you stay true to yourself. What you should focus on instead is improving the kind of treatment that you give to your dad.

Section 9: Use His Language Of Love

How you express your love is what is being referred to by the language of love. As people who do things differently, do not be surprised to find out that you and your dad also have different ways of showing your love for each other. There are five main ways to show someone that you love them. These five main ways are acts of service, words of affirmation, gifts, quality time and physical touch.

One main reason why there is this difference in how we show our love is because the different generations that we belong in. You may be frequently telling your dad that you love him but do not get any words of affirmation in return. Your dad instead keeps cooking food for you which makes you frustrated and this will eventually cause a rift between you two.

So take the time to find out how your dad speaks his language of love. Instead of communicating to your dad how much you love him in your language, do it in his language instead. Does he like to show his love through quality time? If yes then why not start spending more time with him? If he like to get gifts, then give him one every now and then. It does not have to be extravagant. A little something that has meaning for both of you is more than enough. If words of affirmation is his thing then compliment him frequently and tell him how much you love him.

When you speak in your dad's language of love, it is easier for him to see and understand that you love him. He will readily see your intention and will be more than willing to accept that the love that you are showing him. The results will be achieved much faster this way.

Conclusion

When it comes to improving the relationship between you and your dad, remember that the effort should not only come from him. Do not wait for him to make the first move. If you see that he is not doing anything to make things better between the two of you, then take the initiative to improve your relationship. Do not let your pride or ego get in the way. Do not wait for the time when he becomes to ill before you start making things better between you two. And neither should you wait for the time that he passes away. You'll only end up regretting the opportunities that you allowed to pass by and when he is gone, there will be no way to turn the time back to do things differently. So while your dad is still around, start taking the necessary steps to improve your relationship.

If you have any unresolved issues with your father, it is really important that you settle that first. You can have a sincere discussion about the things that are getting in your way and any emotional baggage that you or your father might have. If there are things that you need to forgive him for, find the heart to give him your forgiveness even when it seems like the most difficult thing to do. When you do, you'll be freeing yourself from this pain and it will be easier to move on.

Once you have resolved any issues between the two of you, there are many other ways that you can improve your relationship. You can spend time with him especially during special occasions. It's also important that you and your father have an open communication line so that you can easily catch up with each other. And never ever forget to show your dad that you love him in a way/language that will be easy for him to understand.

www.ingramcontent.com/pod-product-compliance
Lightning Source LLC
Chambersburg PA
CBHW060045040426
42331CB00032B/2478